Do YOU see ME Series

Do YOU see ME at NIGHT?

Written by
Bonnie G. Busbin
Illustrated by Kimberly Courtney

2023
Enjoy!
Miss Bonnie

LANIER PRESS

LANIER PRESS *an Imprint of BookLogix*

Alpharetta, GA

ISBN: 978-1-6653-0625-6 - Paperback
ISBN: 978-1-6653-0626-3 - Hardcover

Library of Congress Control Number: 2023908044

☉This paper meets the requirements of ANSI/NISO Z39.48-1992 (Permanence of Paper)

Editor: Bobbie Hinman
Illustrator: Kimberly Courtney
Chattahoochee Nature Center, Roswell, Georgia: Kim Ellis

References: www.natgeokids.com; www.nationalgeographic.com; dictionary.com

0 5 0 8 2 3

Thank you to my family and friends for their encouragement and support along this journey.
—Bonnie G. Busbin

I am thankful for my greatest blessing, Stella Rose!
—Kimberly Courtney

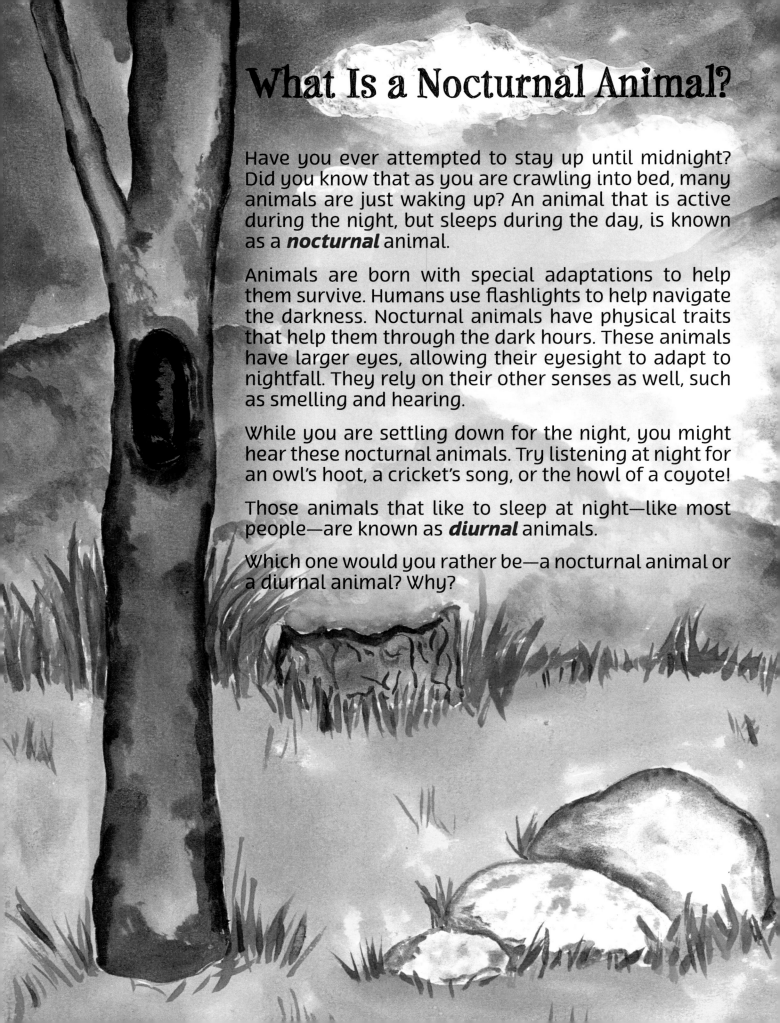

What Is a Nocturnal Animal?

Have you ever attempted to stay up until midnight? Did you know that as you are crawling into bed, many animals are just waking up? An animal that is active during the night, but sleeps during the day, is known as a **nocturnal** animal.

Animals are born with special adaptations to help them survive. Humans use flashlights to help navigate the darkness. Nocturnal animals have physical traits that help them through the dark hours. These animals have larger eyes, allowing their eyesight to adapt to nightfall. They rely on their other senses as well, such as smelling and hearing.

While you are settling down for the night, you might hear these nocturnal animals. Try listening at night for an owl's hoot, a cricket's song, or the howl of a coyote!

Those animals that like to sleep at night—like most people—are known as **diurnal** animals.

Which one would you rather be—a nocturnal animal or a diurnal animal? Why?

Perched high on a branch, my *talons* grip tight.
Eyes wide, I'm in search of a feast for tonight.
With a twist of my head, WHOO WHOO do I see?
A reason for me to come down from this tree.

Do YOU see ME at NIGHT?
What am I?

I am an **OWL**. I quietly fly throughout the night in search of food. I have fixed eye sockets, which means my eyes can only look straight ahead. I can rotate my head nearly all the way around to see things behind me. I rely on my sense of hearing while searching for my *prey* in the darkness.

Upon your first sight, you may think I'm quite cute,
Despite prickly spikes sticking out from my suit.
Turn me loose in your garden, I'll eat all your bugs.
Too bad I'm so spiky, I'm longing for hugs!

Do YOU see ME at NIGHT?

What am I?

I am a **HEDGEHOG.** The prickly spikes that cover my body are long and sharp. I use them to defend myself. My long snout helps me hunt for insects. The "hedge" in my name comes from where I build my nest—near hedges, bushes, and shrubs. The "hog" comes from the grunting and snorting sound I make, like a pig. Hedgehogs are not found in the wild in North America but are primarily found in Africa.

A warm summer night is a favorite of mine.
That's when you will see my outstanding light shine.
Blinking and flashing as bright as a star,
My signal attracts friends from near and from far.

Do YOU see ME at NIGHT?

What am I?

I am a **FIREFLY**. I am a type of beetle; you may know me best as a *lightning bug*. My light is visible once the sun has set during the summer months. I use my light to communicate with other fireflies. Each *species* has its own distinct flashing pattern. If I am eaten by a *predator* (OH MY!), I will release *toxic*, foul-smelling blood that is filled with nasty chemicals. Therefore, the flashing light is a warning sign to birds and lizards to stay away!

At first, I look just like the pet in your home,
But at night my wild instincts say, "Time to go roam."
I have a thick, droopy tail and such wide yellow eyes,
And the howls you hear in the dark are my cries.

Do YOU see ME at NIGHT?

What am I?

I am a **COYOTE**. My size is about the same as a medium-sized dog. By eating *rodents*, I make humans happy. I am fast and intelligent. My howling communicates with other coyotes that I am establishing my territory. I do most of my hunting at night.

With a long stripe of white, and the rest of me black,
I'm not such a difficult creature to track.
My bad reputation cannot be denied.
With a lift of my tail—*PHEW!* Better go hide!

Do YOU see ME at NIGHT?

What am I?

I am a **SKUNK**. As a method of self-defense, I lift my tail and squirt a gross, foul-smelling liquid. The spray is known as *musk* and can cause a terrible odor that may linger for days. The black and white of my coat sends a warning sign to predators to keep away. If you see me lift my tail, you'd better run!

Sneaking in from the cold, squeezing through any space,
I scurry and squeak. Oh, the look on your face!
I've got a pointed brown nose and a long skinny tail.
You can tell where I've been, as I leave you a trail.

Do YOU see ME at NIGHT?

What am I?

I am a **MOUSE**. Give me any small hole and I will figure out how to get into your home. I'm good at hiding, so you might not ever see me. I am looking for warmth and food. I have a large appetite and will eat just about anything. I especially like peanut butter. The *droppings* I leave behind are a good indicator of where I have been.

A rub of my wings is a musical treat . . .
That you may often hear in the summer night's heat.
My ears are quite small, my antennae are long.
Do you think I'm a grasshopper? That would be wrong!

Do YOU see ME at NIGHT?

What am I?

I am a **CRICKET.** As a male cricket, I make music by rubbing the base of my wings together. My ears are among the smallest of all animals. I search for food with my long *antennae*. They enable me to sense and smell objects around me. Lots of animals think I'm delicious, so I must be sure to jump away from snakes, frogs, and rats.

The tip of my tail is as white as the snow.
The rest is all red, as you probably know.
My large ears can hear prey digging under the ground.
Being sly, I can wait without making a sound.

Do YOU see ME at NIGHT?

What am I?

I am a **RED FOX**. My fur is thick, soft, and a rusty red color. My tail has a white tip at the end. I wrap my tail around my body for warmth. My tail can also be used for balance and to communicate to other animals, giving signals that only other foxes understand. My hearing is excellent. I can hear rodents digging for miles, even underground.

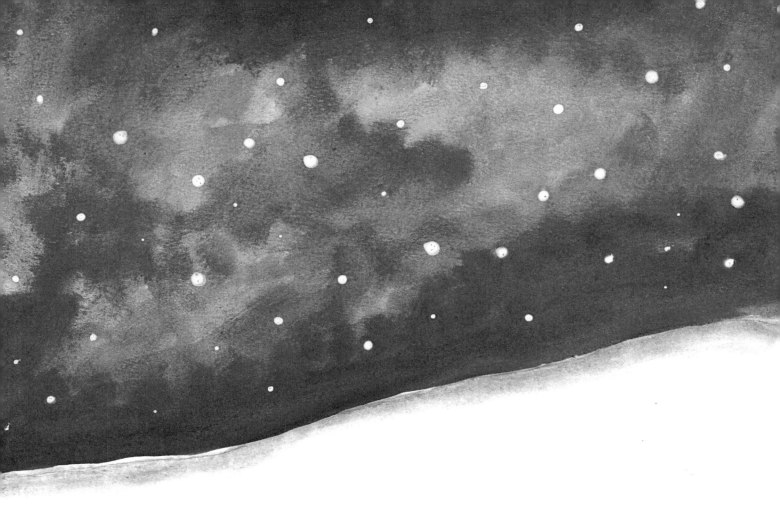

Why say I am scary? I'm useful to all.
I eat lots of insects and yet I am small.
With the sharpest of teeth, in darkness I fly.
I sleep upside down. I'm a real SPOOKY guy.

Do YOU see ME at NIGHT?
What am I?

I am a **BAT**. I have beady little black eyes that can see in the dark. My wings are an extension of the skin from my back and stomach. I have the distinction of being the only *mammal* in the world that can fly. I use *echolocation* when hunting for food at night. Many bats *hibernate* in winter months when insects are difficult to find. I have very sharp, pointed teeth that are used to kill my prey, as well as a set of canines, commonly known as fangs.

The world I inhabit is an underground maze,
With digging—then resting—taking most of my days.
Digging tunnels in search of an earthworm delight,
I can't help that I have such a huge appetite!

Do YOU see ME at NIGHT?

What am I?

I am a **MOLE**. I am the busiest of mammals, searching underground day and night for my favorite meal of earthworms. I have short back legs and longer front legs with large paws that serve as shovels for digging. I hide in my tunnels when predators are nearby.

When I'm young I stick closely to my mother's side,
In her pouch, on her back, just along for the ride.
I play dead when I'm threatened and drop to the ground.
The game stops when my enemy is nowhere around.

Do YOU see ME at NIGHT?

What am I?

I am an **OPOSSUM**. I am the only *marsupial* that originated in the United States. My long tail is almost hairless and serves as a fifth hand for extra support. I am famous for "playing possum" when I am in danger. I pretend to be dead as I drop to the ground. Then my body produces a green liquid that has an awful smell. My predators think I am dead and leave me alone. Surprise, I fooled them!

When the lights on your car shine right into my eyes,
My mask is revealed. It's an awesome disguise!
You may watch as I creep toward your full garbage pail.
I'm the cute, sneaky critter with rings on my tail.

Do YOU see ME at NIGHT?

What am I?

I am a **RACCOON.** I have dark fur around my eyes that makes it look like I'm wearing a mask. This dark fur helps me see clearly as it absorbs the light. I also use my sense of touch to find small animals, insects, and garbage to eat. My paws resemble human hands and are strong enough to untie knots and open doorknobs. The rings on my tail are helpful in allowing me to blend in with my surroundings.

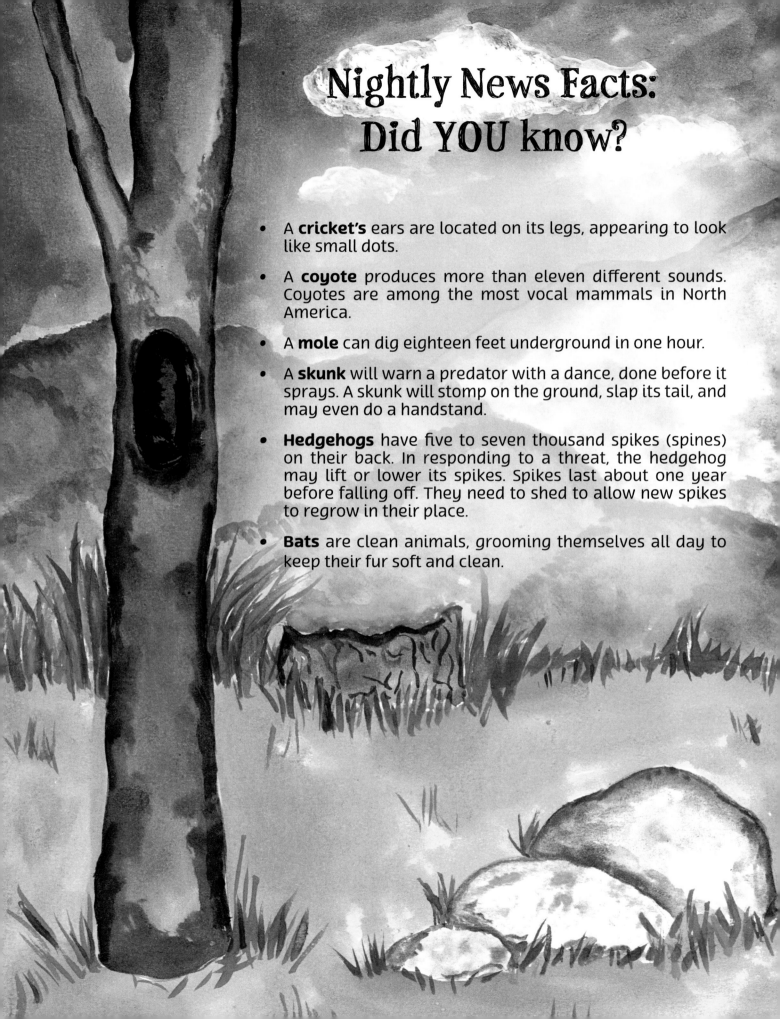

Nightly News Facts: Did YOU know?

- A **cricket's** ears are located on its legs, appearing to look like small dots.

- A **coyote** produces more than eleven different sounds. Coyotes are among the most vocal mammals in North America.

- A **mole** can dig eighteen feet underground in one hour.

- A **skunk** will warn a predator with a dance, done before it sprays. A skunk will stomp on the ground, slap its tail, and may even do a handstand.

- **Hedgehogs** have five to seven thousand spikes (spines) on their back. In responding to a threat, the hedgehog may lift or lower its spikes. Spikes last about one year before falling off. They need to shed to allow new spikes to regrow in their place.

- **Bats** are clean animals, grooming themselves all day to keep their fur soft and clean.

- In some European countries, the female **firefly** is wingless. These nocturnal insects are commonly known as glowworms.

- **Opossums** love to stay in trees as much as possible. However, they are not able to support their weight by hanging from their tail on a tree branch. Their tail does help for balance purposes.

- An **owl** eats its prey whole or in chunks. The owl is not able to digest feathers, bones, and fur. The waste is spit out as a ***pellet.***

- A **mouse** is like a gymnast. It can jump, climb, and swim. A mouse can jump a foot in the air, enabling it to get onto counters—and into your pantry.

- President Calvin Coolidge had a pet **raccoon** named Rebecca. She was free to roam in the White House and was known to unscrew lightbulbs.

- The **red fox** is a very athletic animal. It can jump a fence six feet tall and run up to speeds of thirty miles per hour.

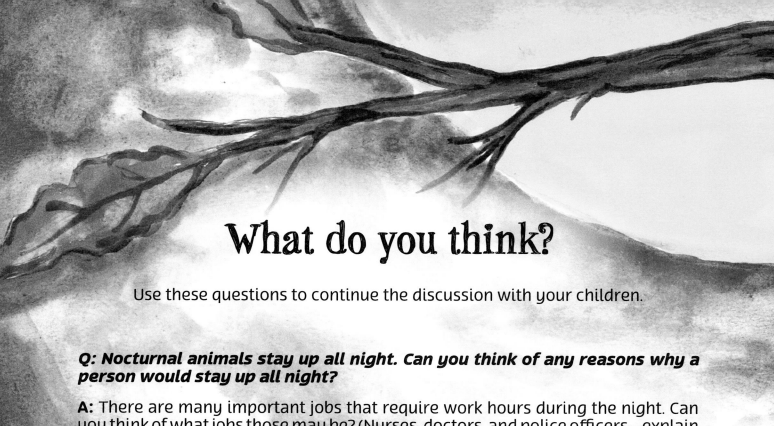

What do you think?

Use these questions to continue the discussion with your children.

Q: *Nocturnal animals stay up all night. Can you think of any reasons why a person would stay up all night?*

A: There are many important jobs that require work hours during the night. Can you think of what jobs those may be? (Nurses, doctors, and police officers—explain why they must be on duty at night.)

Q: *Are you afraid of the dark? Is there anything you can do to help you feel less fearful?*

A: This is a wonderful time to discuss one's fears of the dark and what can help. A special nighttime stuffed animal can help. Also, a nightlight, a flashlight, and knowing the layout of your room can all help you feel safer in the dark.

Q: *Nocturnal animals use their senses to hunt and explore. How do your five senses help you get around when it's dark?*

A: Review the senses: sight, smell, taste, touch, and hearing. Which of these senses might help humans through the dark?

Q: *What are the activities that you perform at night?*

A: Children perform most activities during the daylight hours. Are any of these activities possible to do at night?

New Vocabulary Words

Antennae – a pair of long, thin body parts on the head of insects and other animals, used for feeling and smelling

Diurnal – animals that sleep at night and are active during the daytime hours

Droppings – the food or waste that animals and birds leave behind

Echolocation – emitting sound waves and listening for the echo in order to determine the location of objects

Hibernate – sleeping or staying in one place during the winter months

Mammals – animals with backbones, most of their body covered with hair, and the mother feeding her young with milk from her body

Marsupials – a type of mammal that is born not fully developed and is carried in its mother's pouch until it is ready to be on its own

Musk – a liquid with a strong odor that is released by some animals to keep their predators away

Nocturnal – animals that sleep or rest during the day and are active at night

Pellet – a small wad, or ball, of the remains of an owl's prey that the owl cannot fully digest and therefore spits it up

Predators – an animal or insect that hunts and harms other animals or insects, primarily for food

Prey – an animal or insect hunted and captured for food

Rodent – a small animal that gnaws or nibbles, such as a squirrel, mouse, or rat

Species – a group, or class, of animals having common characteristics

Talons – the sharp claws of a bird of prey

Toxic – a poisonous or harmful substance

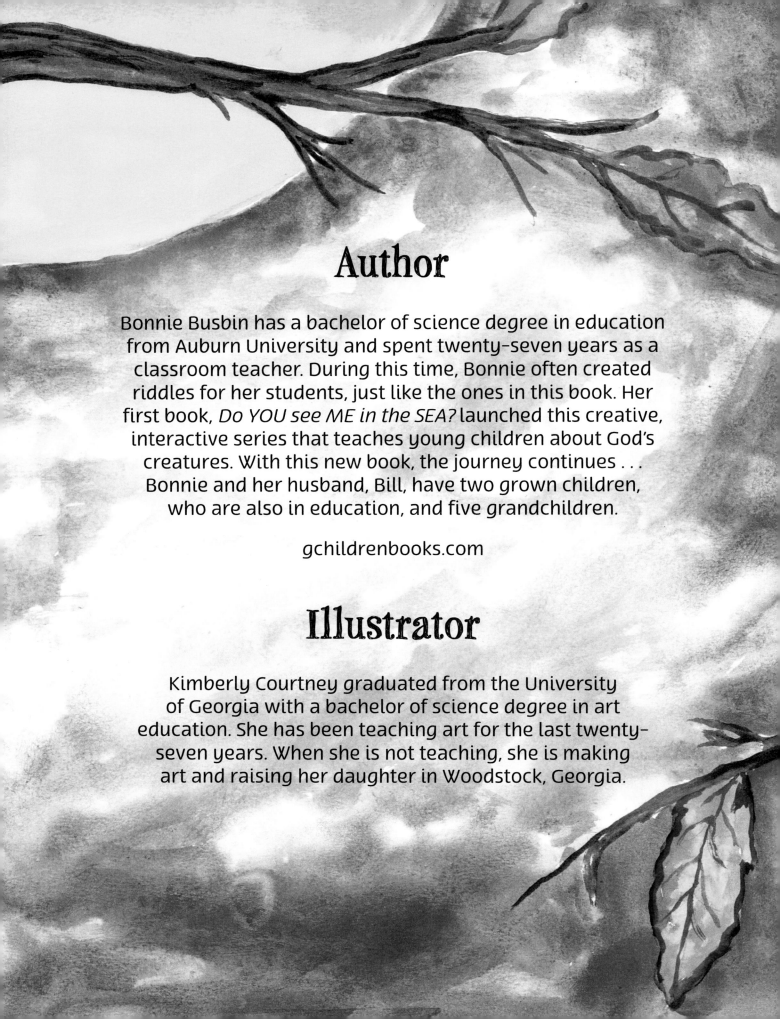

Author

Bonnie Busbin has a bachelor of science degree in education from Auburn University and spent twenty-seven years as a classroom teacher. During this time, Bonnie often created riddles for her students, just like the ones in this book. Her first book, *Do YOU see ME in the SEA?* launched this creative, interactive series that teaches young children about God's creatures. With this new book, the journey continues . . . Bonnie and her husband, Bill, have two grown children, who are also in education, and five grandchildren.

gchildrenbooks.com

Illustrator

Kimberly Courtney graduated from the University of Georgia with a bachelor of science degree in art education. She has been teaching art for the last twenty-seven years. When she is not teaching, she is making art and raising her daughter in Woodstock, Georgia.